NINJA CREAMI HIGH PROTEIN COOKBOOK FOR BEGINNERS

1500 Days of Guilt-Free Frozen Desserts: Master Your CREAMi with Simple, Delicious Recipes for Protein Ice Cream, Sorbet, and Milkshakes to Fuel Your Body and Satisfy Cravings

CONTENTS

CHAPTER 1 INTRODUCTION

Understanding Your Ninja CREAMi

The Ninja CREAMi is more than just an ice cream maker; it is a versatile, high-powered kitchen appliance designed to create smooth, creamy frozen desserts from a variety of bases.

Unlike traditional ice cream machines that churn during freezing, the CREAMi works with a "***freeze then process***" method. You start by preparing a base—such as a high-protein mixture with milk, protein powder, sweetener, and flavorings—and freezing it solid in the included pint container for 24 hours. Once frozen, the CREAMi's specialized blades shave and blend the ice block into a creamy, airy texture.

One of the biggest advantages for health-conscious dessert lovers is its ***adaptability***. The CREAMi is not limited to high-fat, high-sugar bases; it can process lighter, protein-rich recipes without compromising on texture.

Its key functions allow you to ***customize the texture and flavor*** of each creation. The Mix-In feature is especially valuable for incorporating add-ins like nuts, fruit, or protein bites without over-processing them.

Cleaning is also straightforward. The blade, lid, and pint are dishwasher-safe, making it easy to transition between recipes. Because the appliance processes frozen bases in minutes, you can prepare several pints in advance, store them in the freezer, and spin them as needed. This is particularly useful for meal prepping protein desserts.

In short, the Ninja CREAMi gives you full control over ingredients, texture, and flavor, enabling you to enjoy frozen treats that match your dietary goals. With some practice and creativity, it becomes an essential tool for anyone who wants indulgence without sacrificing nutrition.

Choosing the Right Protein Powder

Selecting the right protein powder for frozen desserts depends on your dietary needs and flavor preferences. Here are some popular options:

Whey Protein Isolate:

Whey protein isolate is ideal for creamy ice creams and shakes due to its smooth texture and neutral taste. It dissolves easily and enhances richness, making it a go-to for creamy frozen treats. However, it's dairy-based, so it's not suitable for those who are lactose intolerant or vegan.

Casein Protein:

Casein is thicker and slower to digest, producing a dense, rich texture in desserts like gelato. Its slow digestion makes it perfect for a filling, indulgent treat, though it's also dairy-based.

Plant-Based Proteins:

For dairy-free or vegan options, pea, soy, and rice proteins work well. These may have a more noticeable flavor, but adding flavor enhancers like cocoa powder or vanilla can help mask any earthiness. They may also have a grainier texture, so proper blending is essential.

Sweetened vs. Unsweetened:

Sweetened protein powders reduce the need for added sugars, while unsweetened varieties give you more control over sweetness. Always check ingredient lists for fillers, gums, or sugars that can affect texture in frozen desserts. Choosing the right protein powder ensures your frozen treats are both delicious and aligned with your dietary goals.

The Science of High-Protein Frozen Desserts

Protein is more than a nutrient boost in frozen desserts — it directly influences texture, structure, and creaminess. In high-protein ice creams and sorbets, the ***protein helps bind water and fat***, reducing the size of ice crystals and preventing the mixture from feeling icy. This creates a smoother mouthfeel and more satisfying scoop.

Casein and milk proteins are particularly effective at creating richness because they thicken naturally and emulsify fats evenly. Whey protein produces a lighter, fluffier texture and blends easily into liquid bases, making it an excellent choice for soft, aerated ice cream.

For plant-based or dairy-free recipes, ***pea, soy, or rice proteins*** work well but may require additional balancing. These proteins can be slightly grainy, so pairing them with healthy fats like coconut milk or nut butters, or adding small amounts of stabilizers, helps achieve a creamier texture.

From a nutritional perspective, high-protein desserts are ***ideal for fitness-focused individuals*** and anyone aiming for balanced nutrition. Protein supports muscle repair, increases satiety, and slows sugar absorption, all while turning dessert into a functional food.

The Ninja CREAMi's "freeze then process" method works particularly well with protein bases because it aerates them during spinning. This adds lightness and prevents the dense, chalky texture that sometimes results from protein-heavy mixtures. However, ***balance is essential***. Too much protein without adequate liquid or fat will produce a dry, crumbly texture, while excess liquid can lead to a hard, icy product.

Understanding this balance and experimenting with ratios of protein, fat, and liquid is the foundation for consistently delicious high-protein frozen treats that can rival their traditional, high-sugar counterparts.

Boosting Flavor Without Extra Sugar

Creating delicious, healthy frozen desserts is all about building flavor without relying on refined sugar. Natural, low-calorie sweeteners like stevia, monk fruit, and erythritol offer sweetness without spiking blood sugar, while allowing the other ingredients to shine.

Flavor layering is key. Combining extracts such as vanilla, almond, or coconut with real ingredients — like fresh berries, citrus zest, or spices — creates depth and complexity. For chocolate-based recipes, cocoa powder adds richness, and a touch of instant espresso intensifies the flavor without overpowering it.

Using ***concentrated fruit purees or roasted fruits*** can deliver natural sweetness and a more robust taste. For example, roasting strawberries or peaches caramelizes their sugars and boosts flavor, even without adding sweeteners.

Texture-driven flavors also enhance the eating experience. Toasted nuts, unsweetened shredded coconut, or small chocolate chunks can add crunch and variety. The Ninja CREAMi's Mix-In function makes it easy to add these elements at the right moment, so they maintain their integrity without breaking down.

Herbs and spices can provide unexpected complexity. Fresh mint in a chocolate base, basil with strawberry sorbet, or cinnamon in apple pie ice cream can elevate a dessert from simple to gourmet.

By focusing on high-quality ingredients and pairing flavors thoughtfully, you can create frozen desserts that are both satisfying and health-conscious — proving that indulgence doesn't require sugar overload.

Texture Secrets for Creamy, Healthy Treats

Creating creamy, indulgent frozen desserts without relying on heavy cream or sugar is all about understanding texture control. The Ninja CREAMi makes this easier, but the ingredients you choose and how you use them will determine the final scoop.

1. Balance of Liquids, Fats, and Solids

A smooth texture comes from the right ratio of liquid, fat, and solids. Too much liquid leads to ice crystal formation, while too much solid (protein powder, cocoa, nut butters) can make the dessert dry or chalky.

2. Use Healthy Fats for Smoothness

Healthy fats like coconut milk, avocado, or nut butters act as natural emulsifiers, binding water and preventing large ice crystals. Even small amounts can dramatically improve creaminess in low-fat recipes.

3. Pre-Blending the Base

Before freezing, blend all ingredients thoroughly to evenly distribute protein, fats, and sweeteners. This prevents clumping and ensures every bite has a consistent mouthfeel.

4. Utilize the CREAMi's Re-Spin Feature

If your first spin is slightly icy, the Re-Spin function can transform it into a smoother, softer product. This is especially useful for protein-rich or dairy-free bases that can firm up during freezing.

By focusing on these four techniques, you can create desserts that rival full-fat ice cream in texture while aligning with your health goals. The key is experimenting with ratios, understanding how each ingredient affects texture, and letting the Ninja CREAMi's processing power work for you.

Meal Prep and Storage Tips

Prepping your Ninja CREAMi bases in advance saves time, reduces temptation for less healthy options, and ensures you always have a nutritious dessert ready.

1. Batch Prep for Convenience
Make multiple pint bases at once and freeze them for at least 24 hours before processing. This allows you to enjoy a variety of flavors throughout the week without daily prep work.

2. Label and Date Containers
Write the flavor and freeze date on each pint. Protein-based recipes can keep their quality for up to 3 months, but labeling helps you rotate stock and avoid older batches.

3. Prevent Ice Crystals
Store pints in the coldest part of your freezer and keep them tightly sealed. For added protection, wrap the pint in plastic wrap before placing on the lid to reduce freezer burn.

4. Customize Before Serving
Keep bases plain until you're ready to spin them, then use the Mix-In function for nuts, fruit, or chocolate chips. This keeps mix-ins fresh and maintains their texture.

5. Thaw Slightly for Softer Scoops
If a base has been in the freezer for more than a few weeks, let it sit at room temperature for 2–3 minutes before spinning. This short thaw helps the CREAMi blades work more efficiently and results in a creamier texture.

With a little organization, the Ninja CREAMi can become part of your regular meal prep routine. Preparing pints ahead of time not only makes it easier to stick to your nutrition plan, but also ensures you can satisfy sweet cravings instantly — without compromising your goals.

CHAPTER 2
ICE CREAM RECIPES

Vanilla Bean Protein Cream

Ingredients

1 cup unsweetened almond milk
1 scoop vanilla whey protein powder
1 tablespoon almond butter
1 teaspoon vanilla extract
1–2 tablespoons erythritol or monk fruit sweetener
Pinch of sea salt

Directions

Blend all ingredients together until the mixture is smooth and fully combined.

Pour the mixture into the Ninja CREAMi pint container and seal with the lid.

Freeze the pint upright for a minimum of 24 hours until solid.

Process on the "Lite Ice Cream" setting according to your machine's instructions.

Use the "Re-Spin" function if needed, then serve soft or freeze for 15 minutes for a firmer texture.

1

Ingredients

1 cup unsweetened almond milk
1 scoop vanilla whey protein powder
1 tablespoon cream cheese (softened)
½ cup frozen strawberries
1–2 tablespoons erythritol
2 tablespoons crushed sugar-free graham crackers

2

Strawberry Cheesecake Lite Ice Cream

Directions

Blend milk, protein powder, cream cheese, strawberries, and sweetener until smooth.
Pour into Ninja CREAMi pint, secure the lid, and freeze upright for 24 hours.
Process on the "Lite Ice Cream" function, then check for consistency.
Fold in graham crackers using the Mix-In function for a cheesecake crunch.
Serve immediately for a soft texture or freeze for 15–20 minutes for scoopable firmness.

Ingredients

1 cup unsweetened almond milk
1 scoop chocolate whey protein powder
1 tablespoon cocoa powder
1 tablespoon almond butter
1 tablespoon chopped roasted almonds
1–2 tablespoons monk fruit sweetener

3

Chocolate Almond Crunch Ice Cream

Directions

Blend milk, protein powder, cocoa, almond butter, and sweetener.
Pour into pint and freeze for 24 hours.
Process on "Ice Cream" setting.
Use "Re-Spin" if needed.
Mix in almonds before serving.

4

Peanut Butter Brownie Protein Ice Cream

Ingredients

1 cup unsweetened almond milk
1 scoop chocolate whey protein powder
2 tablespoons peanut butter powder
1 tablespoon cocoa powder
2 tablespoons sugar-free brownie chunks
1–2 tablespoons monk fruit sweetener

Directions

Blend milk, protein powder, peanut butter powder, cocoa, and sweetener until smooth.
Pour the mixture into the Ninja CREAMi pint and secure the lid tightly.
Freeze upright for 24 hours to ensure even processing.
Process on the "Lite Ice Cream" setting, checking texture after the first spin.
Fold in brownie chunks using the Mix-In function, then serve immediately or chill briefly for a firmer scoop.

5

Cinnamon Roll Protein Cream

Ingredients

1 cup unsweetened oat milk
1 scoop vanilla whey protein powder
1 teaspoon cinnamon
1 tablespoon almond butter
1–2 tablespoons maple-flavored monk fruit sweetener
1 teaspoon vanilla extract

Directions

Blend oat milk, protein powder, cinnamon, almond butter, sweetener, and vanilla until smooth.
Pour mixture into the Ninja CREAMi pint container and secure the lid.
Place the pint upright in the freezer and freeze for 24 hours.
Process using the "Lite Ice Cream" function, checking texture after the spin.
If needed, use "Re-Spin," then serve topped with a sprinkle of cinnamon or freeze for a firmer dessert.

Salted Caramel Pretzel Crunch

Ingredients

1 cup unsweetened almond milk
1 scoop caramel-flavored whey protein powder
1 tablespoon almond butter
1–2 tablespoons monk fruit sweetener
1 teaspoon caramel extract
2 tablespoons crushed pretzels

Directions

Blend almond milk, protein powder, almond butter, sweetener, and caramel extract until combined.
Pour mixture into the Ninja CREAMi pint and secure the lid.
Freeze upright for at least 24 hours to ensure full solidification.
Process on the "Ice Cream" setting, checking for smoothness.
Add pretzels using the Mix-In function, then serve soft or freeze for 10–15 minutes for a firmer dessert.

6

7

Mocha Espresso Protein Cream

Ingredients

1 cup unsweetened almond milk
1 scoop chocolate whey protein powder
1 tablespoon cocoa powder
1 teaspoon instant espresso powder
1–2 tablespoons monk fruit sweetener

Directions

Blend almond milk, protein powder, cocoa, espresso powder, and sweetener until smooth.
Transfer to Ninja CREAMi pint container and close the lid securely.
Freeze upright for a minimum of 24 hours before processing.
Use the "Lite Ice Cream" setting and check texture after first spin.
Use "Re-Spin" if necessary, then serve with a light dusting of cocoa powder for garnish.

8

Blueberry Muffin Ice Cream

Ingredients

1 cup unsweetened almond milk
1 scoop vanilla whey protein powder
½ cup frozen blueberries
1 teaspoon vanilla extract
1–2 tablespoons erythritol
2 tablespoons sugar-free muffin pieces

Directions

Blend milk, protein powder, blueberries, vanilla, and sweetener until smooth.
Pour mixture into the Ninja CREAMi pint and seal with lid.
Freeze upright for 24 hours in the coldest freezer section.
Process on the "Lite Ice Cream" setting and check consistency.
Fold in muffin pieces using Mix-In, then serve immediately or freeze briefly for firmer texture.

9

Maple Pecan Protein Cream

Ingredients

1 cup unsweetened almond milk
1 scoop vanilla whey protein powder
1 tablespoon almond butter
1 teaspoon maple extract
1–2 tablespoons monk fruit sweetener
2 tablespoons chopped pecans

Directions

Blend almond milk, protein powder, almond butter, maple extract, and sweetener until smooth.
Pour mixture into Ninja CREAMi pint container and secure the lid.
Freeze upright for at least 24 hours until solid.
Process on "Lite Ice Cream" mode, checking texture after first spin.
Fold in pecans using the Mix-In function, then serve soft or after a short freezer chill.

10

Birthday Cake Sprinkle Delightx

Ingredients

1 cup unsweetened almond milk
1 scoop vanilla whey protein powder
1 teaspoon vanilla extract
1–2 tablespoons erythritol
1 tablespoon sugar-free sprinkles

Directions

Blend almond milk, protein powder, vanilla extract, and sweetener until smooth.
Pour mixture into Ninja CREAMi pint and close the lid securely.
Freeze upright for 24 hours before processing.
Process using the "Ice Cream" setting and check consistency after the spin.
Fold in sprinkles using Mix-In, then serve immediately or freeze for 10 minutes for scoopable texture.

11

Cookies & Cream Power Pint

Ingredients

1 cup unsweetened almond milk
1 scoop vanilla whey protein powder
1 tablespoon almond butter
1–2 tablespoons monk fruit sweetener
3 sugar-free chocolate sandwich cookies, chopped

Directions

Blend almond milk, protein powder, almond butter, and sweetener until smooth.
Pour mixture into Ninja CREAMi pint container and secure the lid.
Freeze upright for 24 hours before processing.
Process on "Lite Ice Cream" mode and check texture after the spin.
Fold in chopped cookies using Mix-In, then serve soft or after a short freezer chill.

12

Pistachio White Chocolate Ice Cream

Ingredients

1 cup unsweetened almond milk
1 scoop vanilla whey protein powder
1 teaspoon pistachio extract
1–2 tablespoons erythritol
2 tablespoons chopped pistachios
1 tablespoon sugar-free white chocolate chips

Directions

Blend almond milk, protein powder, pistachio extract, and sweetener until smooth.
Pour mixture into Ninja CREAMi pint and close the lid securely.
Freeze upright for 24 hours before processing.
Use "Ice Cream" setting, checking texture after the first spin.
Fold in pistachios and white chocolate using Mix-In, then serve immediately.

Chocolate Raspberry Truffle Cream

Ingredients

1 cup unsweetened almond milk
1 scoop chocolate whey protein powder
1 tablespoon cocoa powder
1–2 tablespoons monk fruit sweetener
½ cup frozen raspberries
2 tablespoons sugar-free dark chocolate chunks

Directions

Blend almond milk, protein powder, cocoa, raspberries, and sweetener until smooth.
Pour mixture into Ninja CREAMi pint and seal with the lid.
Freeze upright for at least 24 hours before processing.
Process on "Lite Ice Cream" mode and check consistency.
Mix in dark chocolate chunks using Mix-In, then serve immediately.

14

Tiramisu Protein Ice Cream

Ingredients

1 cup unsweetened almond milk
1 scoop vanilla whey protein powder
1 tablespoon cocoa powder
1 teaspoon instant espresso powder
1–2 tablespoons monk fruit sweetener
2 tablespoons crushed sugar-free ladyfingers

Directions

Blend almond milk, protein powder, cocoa, espresso powder, and sweetener until smooth.
Pour mixture into Ninja CREAMi pint and close the lid.
Freeze upright for a full 24 hours.
Process on "Ice Cream" setting and check texture.
Fold in ladyfingers using Mix-In, then dust with cocoa powder before serving.

15

Peanut Butter & Jelly Swirl

Ingredients

1 cup unsweetened almond milk
1 scoop vanilla whey protein powder
1 tablespoon peanut butter
1–2 tablespoons monk fruit sweetener
2 tablespoons sugar-free berry jam

Directions

Blend almond milk, protein powder, peanut butter, and sweetener until smooth.
Pour into Ninja CREAMi pint container and secure the lid.
Freeze upright for at least 24 hours before processing.
Process on "Lite Ice Cream" mode, checking texture after first spin.
Swirl in jam by hand after processing, then serve immediately.

16

Double Chocolate Chip Crunch

Ingredients

1 cup unsweetened almond milk
1 scoop chocolate whey protein powder
1 tablespoon cocoa powder
1–2 tablespoons monk fruit sweetener
2 tablespoons sugar-free chocolate chips

Directions

Blend almond milk, protein powder, cocoa, and sweetener until smooth.
Pour mixture into Ninja CREAMi pint and seal with lid.
Freeze for 24 hours in the coldest part of the freezer.
Process on "Ice Cream" setting and check texture.
Fold in chocolate chips using Mix-In, then serve immediately.

17

Matcha Honeydew Ice Cream

Ingredients

1 cup unsweetened almond milk
1 scoop vanilla whey protein powder
1 teaspoon matcha green tea powder
½ cup diced frozen honeydew melon
1–2 tablespoons erythritol

Directions

Blend almond milk, protein powder, matcha, honeydew, and sweetener until smooth.
Pour into Ninja CREAMi pint and close lid tightly.
Freeze upright for at least 24 hours before spinning.
Process on "Lite Ice Cream" mode, checking consistency.
Serve soft immediately or freeze 10–15 minutes for firmer scoops.

18

Apple Pie à la Mode Cream

Ingredients

1 cup unsweetened almond milk
1 scoop vanilla whey protein powder
½ cup diced frozen apple
1 teaspoon cinnamon
1–2 tablespoons monk fruit sweetener
2 tablespoons crushed sugar-free graham crackers

Directions

Blend almond milk, protein powder, apple, cinnamon, and sweetener until smooth.
Pour into Ninja CREAMi pint and seal with lid.
Freeze upright for 24 hours before processing.
Process on "Lite Ice Cream" setting and check texture.
Fold in graham crackers using Mix-In, then serve.

19

Coconut Almond Bliss

Ingredients

1 cup unsweetened coconut milk
1 scoop vanilla whey protein powder
1 tablespoon almond butter
1–2 tablespoons monk fruit sweetener
2 tablespoons unsweetened shredded coconut
1 tablespoon sliced almonds

Directions

Blend coconut milk, protein powder, almond butter, and sweetener until smooth.
Pour mixture into Ninja CREAMi pint container and secure lid.
Freeze upright for at least 24 hours before spinning.
Process on "Ice Cream" mode and check texture.
Mix in shredded coconut and almonds, then serve.

Banana Cream Pie Lite Ice Cream

Ingredients

1 cup unsweetened almond milk
1 scoop vanilla whey protein powder
½ medium ripe banana
1 teaspoon vanilla extract
1–2 tablespoons erythritol
2 tablespoons crushed sugar-free graham crackers

Directions

Blend almond milk, protein powder, banana, vanilla, and sweetener until smooth.
Pour mixture into Ninja CREAMi pint and secure the lid tightly.
Freeze upright for 24 hours before spinning.
Process on "Lite Ice Cream" mode, checking texture after first spin.
Fold in graham crackers using Mix-In, then serve soft or after a brief freezer chill.

20

21

Rocky Road Protein Cream

Ingredients

1 cup unsweetened almond milk
1 scoop chocolate whey protein powder
1 tablespoon cocoa powder
1–2 tablespoons monk fruit sweetener
2 tablespoons sugar-free marshmallows
2 tablespoons chopped walnuts

Directions

Blend almond milk, protein powder, cocoa, and sweetener until smooth.
Pour into Ninja CREAMi pint container and secure lid.
Freeze upright for a full 24 hours.
Process on "Ice Cream" setting and check texture.
Add marshmallows and walnuts using Mix-In, then serve immediately.

22

Peach Cobbler Ice Cream

Ingredients

Ingredients
1 cup unsweetened almond milk
1 scoop vanilla whey protein powder
½ cup frozen peaches
1–2 tablespoons erythritol
2 tablespoons crushed sugar-free graham crackers

Directions

Blend almond milk, protein powder, peaches, and sweetener until smooth.
Pour into Ninja CREAMi pint and close lid tightly.
Freeze upright for 24 hours before spinning.
Process on "Lite Ice Cream" mode and check consistency.
Fold in graham crackers using Mix-In, then serve.

23

Black Forest Cherry Cream

Ingredients

1 cup unsweetened almond milk
1 scoop chocolate whey protein powder
½ cup frozen cherries
1 tablespoon cocoa powder
1–2 tablespoons monk fruit sweetener
2 tablespoons sugar-free chocolate chunks

Directions

Blend almond milk, protein powder, cherries, cocoa, and sweetener until smooth.
Pour into Ninja CREAMi pint and secure lid.
Freeze upright for 24 hours before processing.
Process on "Ice Cream" mode, checking texture.
Fold in chocolate chunks using Mix-In, then serve.

24

Mint Chocolate Chip Power Cream

Ingredients

1 cup unsweetened almond milk
1 scoop vanilla whey protein powder
½ teaspoon peppermint extract
1–2 tablespoons erythritol
2 tablespoons sugar-free chocolate chips
Green food coloring (optional)

Directions

Blend almond milk, protein powder, peppermint extract, sweetener, and coloring until smooth.
Pour into Ninja CREAMi pint container and secure lid.
Freeze upright for 24 hours before spinning.
Process on "Ice Cream" setting and check texture.
Fold in chocolate chips using Mix-In, then serve immediately.

Pumpkin Pie Spice Ice Cream

Ingredients

1 cup unsweetened almond milk
1 scoop vanilla whey protein powder
¼ cup pumpkin puree
1 teaspoon pumpkin pie spice
1–2 tablespoons monk fruit sweetener

Directions

Blend almond milk, protein powder, pumpkin puree, spice, and sweetener until smooth.
Pour mixture into Ninja CREAMi pint and secure the lid tightly.
Freeze upright for 24 hours before spinning.
Process on "Lite Ice Cream" mode and check texture.
Serve immediately or freeze for 15 minutes for firmer scoops.

CHAPTER 3 GELATO RECIPES

26

Mocha Hazelnut Gelato

Ingredients

- 1 cup unsweetened almond milk
- 1 scoop chocolate whey protein powder
- 1 tablespoon cocoa powder
- 1 teaspoon instant espresso powder
- 1–2 tablespoons monk fruit sweetener
- 2 tablespoons chopped hazelnuts

Directions

Blend almond milk, protein powder, cocoa, espresso powder, and sweetener until smooth.

Pour mixture into Ninja CREAMi pint and secure lid tightly.

Freeze upright for 24 hours before processing.

Process on "Gelato" mode and check texture.

Fold in hazelnuts using Mix-In, then serve immediately.

27

Pistachio Cardamom Gelato

Ingredients

- 1 cup unsweetened almond milk
- 1 scoop vanilla whey protein powder
- 1 teaspoon pistachio extract
- ½ teaspoon ground cardamom
- 1–2 tablespoons erythritol
- 2 tablespoons chopped pistachios

Directions

Blend almond milk, protein powder, pistachio extract, cardamom, and sweetener until smooth.

Pour into Ninja CREAMi pint and secure lid.

Freeze upright for 24 hours before spinning.

Process on "Gelato" mode and check consistency.

Fold in pistachios using Mix-In, then serve immediately.

Coconut Macaroon Gelato

Ingredients

1 cup unsweetened coconut milk
1 scoop vanilla whey protein powder
1–2 tablespoons monk fruit sweetener
2 tablespoons unsweetened shredded coconut
1 teaspoon vanilla extract

Directions

Blend coconut milk, protein powder, sweetener, coconut, and vanilla until smooth.
Pour into Ninja CREAMi pint and seal lid tightly.
Freeze upright for 24 hours before processing.
Process on "Gelato" setting and check texture.
Serve immediately or freeze for 10 minutes for firmer consistency.

29

Dark Chocolate Espresso Gelato

Ingredients

1 cup unsweetened almond milk
1 scoop chocolate whey protein powder
1 tablespoon cocoa powder
1 teaspoon instant espresso powder
1–2 tablespoons monk fruit sweetener

Directions

Blend almond milk, protein powder, cocoa, espresso powder, and sweetener until smooth.
Pour mixture into Ninja CREAMi pint and secure lid.
Freeze upright for 24 hours before spinning.
Process on "Gelato" mode and check texture.
Serve immediately or chill briefly for firmness.

30

Lemon Blueberry Swirl Gelato

Ingredients

1 cup unsweetened almond milk
1 scoop vanilla whey protein powder
1 teaspoon lemon zest
1–2 tablespoons erythritol
½ cup frozen blueberries

Directions

Blend almond milk, protein powder, lemon zest, and sweetener until smooth.
Pour into Ninja CREAMi pint and close lid securely.
Freeze upright for 24 hours before spinning.
Process on "Gelato" mode and check texture.
Swirl in blueberries after processing, then serve.

Strawberry Basil Gelato

Ingredients

1 cup unsweetened almond milk
1 scoop vanilla whey protein powder
½ cup frozen strawberries
3 fresh basil leaves
1–2 tablespoons erythritol

Directions

Blend almond milk, protein powder, strawberries, basil, and sweetener until smooth.
Pour into Ninja CREAMi pint and close lid.
Freeze upright for 24 hours before spinning.
Process on "Gelato" mode and check consistency.
Serve immediately for a refreshing flavor.

32

Almond Toffee Gelato

Ingredients

1 cup unsweetened almond milk
1 scoop vanilla whey protein powder
1 teaspoon almond extract
1–2 tablespoons monk fruit sweetener
2 tablespoons sugar-free toffee bits

Directions

Blend almond milk, protein powder, almond extract, and sweetener until smooth.
Pour mixture into Ninja CREAMi pint and secure lid.
Freeze upright for 24 hours before spinning.
Process on "Gelato" mode and check texture.
Fold in toffee bits using Mix-In, then serve.

33

Mango Ginger Gelato

Ingredients

1 cup unsweetened almond milk
1 scoop vanilla whey protein powder
½ cup frozen mango chunks
½ teaspoon ground ginger
1–2 tablespoons erythritol

Directions

Blend almond milk, protein powder, mango, ginger, and sweetener until smooth.
Pour into Ninja CREAMi pint and close lid.
Freeze upright for 24 hours before spinning.
Process on "Gelato" mode and check texture.
Serve soft or freeze briefly for firmer scoops.

Maple Walnut Gelato

Ingredients

1 cup unsweetened almond milk
1 scoop vanilla whey protein powder
1 teaspoon maple extract
1–2 tablespoons monk fruit sweetener
2 tablespoons chopped walnuts

Directions

Blend almond milk, protein powder, maple extract, and sweetener until smooth and well mixed.
Transfer the base into the Ninja CREAMi pint, leaving a small gap at the top.
Freeze the pint upright for 24 hours or until fully solid.
Use the "Gelato" setting to process until creamy and evenly textured.
Fold in walnuts with the Mix-In function, then serve immediately for the best flavor and texture.

35

Salted Caramel Latte Gelato

Ingredients

1 cup unsweetened almond milk
1 scoop caramel-flavored whey protein powder
1 teaspoon instant coffee
1–2 tablespoons monk fruit sweetener
Pinch of sea salt

Directions

Blend almond milk, protein powder, coffee, sweetener, and salt until smooth.
Pour mixture into Ninja CREAMi pint and secure lid tightly.
Freeze upright for at least 24 hours.
Process on "Gelato" mode and check texture.
Serve immediately or chill slightly before serving.

36

Vanilla Fig Gelato

Ingredients

1 cup unsweetened almond milk
1 scoop vanilla whey protein powder
2 dried figs, chopped
1 teaspoon vanilla extract
1–2 tablespoons erythritol

Directions

Combine almond milk, protein powder, figs, vanilla, and sweetener in a blender and blend until silky smooth.
Pour the mixture into your Ninja CREAMi pint container, making sure not to overfill it.
Freeze upright for at least 24 hours so the base solidifies completely.
Process using the "Gelato" setting until creamy and well-aerated.
Serve immediately for a soft texture, or place in the freezer for 15 minutes for a firmer scoop.

37

Peanut Butter Banana Gelato

Ingredients

1 cup unsweetened almond milk
1 scoop vanilla whey protein powder
1 tablespoon peanut butter
½ ripe banana
1–2 tablespoons monk fruit sweetener

Directions

Blend almond milk, protein powder, peanut butter, banana, and sweetener until fully combined and smooth in texture.
Transfer the mixture to the Ninja CREAMi pint container, leaving a small gap at the top.
Freeze the pint in an upright position for a minimum of 24 hours.
Use the “Gelato” mode to process until it reaches a rich, creamy consistency.
Serve immediately or return to the freezer for a short chill to firm it slightly.

38

Raspberry Almond Gelato

Ingredients

1 cup unsweetened almond milk
1 scoop vanilla whey protein powder
½ cup frozen raspberries
1 teaspoon almond extract
1–2 tablespoons erythritol

Directions

Blend almond milk, protein powder, raspberries, almond extract, and sweetener until smooth.
Pour the mixture into the Ninja CREAMi pint, ensuring it is evenly distributed.
Place the pint upright in your freezer for 24 hours or longer if needed.
Process on “Gelato” mode until smooth, stopping to scrape down the sides if necessary.
Serve immediately for a softer treat or freeze briefly to achieve a more solid texture.

39

Honey Lavender Gelato

Ingredients

1 cup unsweetened almond milk
1 scoop vanilla whey protein powder
1 teaspoon dried culinary lavender
1 tablespoon honey or sugar-free honey alternative
1–2 tablespoons erythritol

Directions

Blend almond milk, protein powder, lavender, honey, and sweetener until the mixture is smooth and fragrant.
Transfer to a Ninja CREAMi pint container, being careful not to overfill the container.
Freeze the mixture in an upright position for 24 hours to set fully.
Run the "Gelato" program to process until creamy and smooth.
Serve right away or freeze an additional 10–15 minutes for a denser texture.

40

Matcha White Chocolate Gelato

Ingredients

1 cup unsweetened almond milk
1 scoop vanilla whey protein powder
1 teaspoon matcha powder
1–2 tablespoons erythritol
2 tablespoons sugar-free white chocolate chips

Directions

Blend almond milk, protein powder, matcha, and sweetener until evenly combined with a consistent green color.
Pour into the Ninja CREAMi pint, making sure to leave room for expansion during freezing.
Freeze for at least 24 hours with the pint in an upright position. Then process on the "Gelato" setting until the mixture becomes creamy and smooth.
Add white chocolate chips using the Mix-In function and serve.

Chocolate Mint Gelato

Ingredients

1 cup unsweetened almond milk
1 scoop chocolate whey protein powder
1 tablespoon cocoa powder
½ teaspoon peppermint extract
1–2 tablespoons monk fruit sweetener
2 tablespoons sugar-free chocolate chips (Mix-In)

Directions

Blend almond milk, protein powder, cocoa powder, peppermint extract, and sweetener until completely smooth.
Pour the mixture into your Ninja CREAMi pint container, leaving a little space at the top for expansion.
Freeze upright for at least 24 hours until solid.
Process on the "Gelato" setting until smooth and creamy.
Fold in chocolate chips using the Mix-In function, then serve for a cool, high-protein, low-sugar treat.

CHAPTER 4
MILKSHAKE RECIPES

Strawberry Oat Protein Shake

Ingredients

1 cup unsweetened oat milk
1 scoop vanilla whey protein powder
½ cup frozen strawberries
2 tablespoons rolled oats
1–2 tablespoons erythritol
½ cup ice cubes

Directions

Combine oat milk, protein powder, strawberries, oats, sweetener, and ice in a blender.
Blend on high until the mixture is smooth, thick, and evenly pink throughout.
Taste and adjust sweetness, blending briefly if adding more.
Pour into a tall glass for a refreshing, fiber-rich shake.
Enjoy immediately while cold for the freshest strawberry flavor and perfect creamy texture

Salted Caramel Mocha Shake

Ingredients

1 cup unsweetened almond milk
1 scoop chocolate whey protein powder
1 teaspoon instant espresso powder
1 teaspoon caramel extract
1–2 tablespoons monk fruit sweetener
½ cup ice cubes

Directions

Add almond milk, protein powder, espresso powder, caramel extract, sweetener, and ice to a blender.
Blend until smooth, thick, and fully combined with a rich mocha color.
Taste and adjust sweetness or caramel flavor if desired, blending again briefly.
Pour into a chilled glass for the most refreshing presentation.
Serve immediately for a decadent yet balanced protein-packed coffeehouse-style shake.

44

Blueberry Cheesecake Shake

Ingredients

1 cup unsweetened almond milk
1 scoop vanilla whey protein powder
½ cup frozen blueberries
1 tablespoon cream cheese (softened)
1–2 tablespoons erythritol
½ cup ice cubes

Directions

Place almond milk, protein powder, blueberries, cream cheese, sweetener, and ice into a blender.
Blend until the mixture is creamy, thick, and evenly colored.
Adjust sweetness as needed, blending again if more is added.
Pour into a glass and garnish with extra blueberries if desired.
Serve immediately for a dessert-like shake with cheesecake richness and fruity brightness.

45

Cookies & Cream Recovery Shake

Ingredients

1 cup unsweetened almond milk
1 scoop vanilla whey protein powder
2 sugar-free chocolate sandwich cookies
1–2 tablespoons monk fruit sweetener
½ cup ice cubes

Directions

Add almond milk, protein powder, cookies, sweetener, and ice cubes to a blender.
Blend on high until smooth, creamy, and speckled with cookie bits throughout.
Check for sweetness and adjust if desired, blending again briefly.
Pour into a tall glass for a treat-like recovery drink.
Serve immediately while cold for a satisfying post-workout indulgence.

46

Mint Mocha Shake

Ingredients

1 cup unsweetened almond milk
1 scoop chocolate whey protein powder
1 teaspoon instant espresso powder
½ teaspoon peppermint extract
1–2 tablespoons monk fruit sweetener
½ cup ice cubes

Directions

Combine almond milk, protein powder, espresso powder, peppermint extract, sweetener, and ice in a blender.
Blend on high until creamy, frothy, and fully combined.
Taste and adjust sweetness or mint flavor if needed, blending again briefly.
Pour into a chilled glass for the best temperature and presentation.
Serve immediately for a cool, energizing shake with a refreshing mocha twist.

47

Banana Almond Breakfast Shake

Ingredients

1 cup unsweetened almond milk
1 scoop vanilla whey protein powder
1 ripe banana
1 tablespoon almond butter
1–2 tablespoons erythritol
½ cup ice cubes

Directions

Add almond milk, protein powder, banana, almond butter, sweetener, and ice to a blender.
Blend until smooth, thick, and creamy.
Taste and adjust sweetness if desired, blending again briefly.
Pour into a tall glass for a hearty, satisfying breakfast option.
Serve immediately for the best flavor and texture.

Matcha Coconut Shake

Ingredients

1 cup unsweetened coconut milk
1 scoop vanilla whey protein powder
1 teaspoon matcha powder
1–2 tablespoons monk fruit sweetener
½ cup ice cubes

Directions

Combine coconut milk, protein powder, matcha powder, sweetener, and ice in a blender.
Blend until creamy, smooth, and evenly green in color.
Taste and adjust sweetness if needed, blending briefly again.
Pour into a chilled glass for a bright, refreshing shake.
Serve immediately for the freshest taste and texture.

48

Ingredients

1 cup unsweetened almond milk
1 scoop vanilla whey protein powder
½ teaspoon cinnamon
1 teaspoon vanilla extract
1–2 tablespoons monk fruit sweetener
½ cup ice cubes

49

Vanilla Cinnamon Shake

Directions

Combine almond milk, protein powder, cinnamon, vanilla extract, sweetener, and ice in a blender.
Blend until smooth, thick, and creamy.
Adjust sweetness if desired, blending again briefly.
Pour into a glass for a lightly spiced, warming shake.
Serve immediately for best flavor and consistency.

Ingredients

1 cup unsweetened almond milk
1 scoop vanilla whey protein powder
¼ cup pumpkin puree
½ teaspoon pumpkin pie spice
1 teaspoon instant coffee
1–2 tablespoons monk fruit sweetener
½ cup ice cubes

50

Pumpkin Spice Latte Shake

Directions

Add almond milk, protein powder, pumpkin puree, spice, coffee, sweetener, and ice to a blender.
Blend until smooth, thick, and evenly mixed.
Taste and adjust sweetness if desired.
Pour into a tall glass for a seasonal, protein-packed latte treat.
Serve immediately for the freshest taste.

51

Almond Joy Shake

Ingredients

1 cup unsweetened coconut milk
1 scoop chocolate whey protein powder
1 tablespoon almond butter
1 tablespoon unsweetened shredded coconut
1–2 tablespoons monk fruit sweetener
½ cup ice cubes

Directions

Combine coconut milk, protein powder, almond butter, shredded coconut, sweetener, and ice in a blender.
Blend until smooth, creamy, and fully combined.
Taste and adjust sweetness if needed, blending again briefly.
Pour into a chilled glass for a dessert-like shake.
Serve immediately for the best flavor and texture.

52

Peanut Butter Pretzel Shake

Ingredients

1 cup unsweetened almond milk
1 scoop vanilla whey protein powder
1 tablespoon peanut butter
1–2 tablespoons monk fruit sweetener
2 tablespoons crushed pretzels
½ cup ice cubes

Directions

Add almond milk, protein powder, peanut butter, sweetener, pretzels, and ice to a blender.
Blend until smooth but still with slight pretzel texture for crunch.
Taste and adjust sweetness if desired.
Pour into a glass and top with extra pretzels if preferred.
Serve immediately for sweet and salty satisfaction.

53

Mocha Chia Shake

Ingredients

1 cup unsweetened almond milk
1 scoop chocolate whey protein powder
1 teaspoon instant espresso powder
1 tablespoon chia seeds
1–2 tablespoons monk fruit sweetener
½ cup ice cubes

Directions

Combine almond milk, protein powder, espresso powder, chia seeds, sweetener, and ice in a blender.
Blend until creamy and well mixed, allowing chia seeds to add texture.
Taste and adjust sweetness if needed.
Pour into a glass for a high-fiber, energizing shake.
Serve immediately for best consistency.

54

Raspberry White Chocolate Shake

Ingredients

1 cup unsweetened almond milk
1 scoop vanilla whey protein powder
½ cup frozen raspberries
1 tablespoon sugar-free white chocolate chips
1–2 tablespoons erythritol
½ cup ice cubes

Directions

Add almond milk, protein powder, raspberries, white chocolate chips, sweetener, and ice to a blender.
Blend until thick, creamy, and pink with small chocolate flecks.
Taste and adjust sweetness if desired.
Pour into a glass and garnish with extra raspberries if preferred.
Serve immediately for a fruity, indulgent treat.

Chocolate Cherry Shake

Ingredients

1 cup unsweetened almond milk
1 scoop chocolate whey protein powder
½ cup frozen cherries
1–2 tablespoons erythritol
½ cup ice cubes

Directions

Add almond milk, protein powder, cherries, sweetener, and ice to a blender.
Blend until thick, smooth, and evenly mixed.
Taste and adjust sweetness if desired.
Pour into a glass and garnish with a cherry on top if preferred.
Serve immediately for a rich, fruity chocolate treat.

CHAPTER 5 SMOOTHIE BOWL RECIPES

56

Tropical Paradise Smoothie Bowl

Ingredients

½ cup unsweetened almond milk
1 scoop vanilla whey protein powder
½ cup frozen mango chunks
½ cup frozen pineapple chunks
1–2 tablespoons erythritol
¼ cup shredded coconut (for topping)

Directions

Blend almond milk, protein powder, mango, pineapple, and sweetener until thick and creamy.
Pour into a bowl, spreading evenly for a smooth base.
Top with shredded coconut for a tropical flavor boost.
Add extra mango or pineapple if desired for presentation.
Serve immediately with a spoon for best taste and texture.

57

Chocolate Peanut Butter Crunch Bowl

Ingredients

½ cup unsweetened almond milk
1 scoop chocolate whey protein powder
1 tablespoon peanut butter
1 tablespoon cocoa powder
1–2 tablespoons monk fruit sweetener
¼ cup granola (for topping)

Directions

Blend almond milk, protein powder, peanut butter, cocoa powder, and sweetener until thick and smooth.
Transfer to a serving bowl, spreading evenly.
Sprinkle granola over the top for crunch and texture.
Add banana slices for extra sweetness if desired.
Serve immediately for a filling, dessert-like breakfast or snack.

Acai Berry Protein Bowl

Ingredients

½ cup unsweetened almond milk
1 scoop vanilla whey protein powder
1 packet frozen acai puree (unsweetened)
½ cup frozen mixed berries
1–2 tablespoons erythritol
¼ cup granola (for topping)

Directions

Blend almond milk, protein powder, acai puree, berries, and sweetener until thick.
Scoop into a bowl, smoothing the surface.
Top with granola for crunch and fiber.
Garnish with extra berries for presentation.
Serve immediately to keep the toppings crisp.

59

Green Power Detox Bowl

Ingredients

½ cup unsweetened almond milk
1 scoop vanilla whey protein powder
½ frozen banana
½ cup frozen spinach
½ cup frozen pineapple chunks
1–2 tablespoons monk fruit sweetener

Directions

Blend almond milk, protein powder, banana, spinach, pineapple, and sweetener until vibrant green and creamy.
Pour into a bowl and level the surface.
Top with chia seeds or pumpkin seeds for added nutrition.
Garnish with pineapple chunks for a sweet finish.
Serve immediately while cold for a refreshing boost.

60

Berry Coconut Crunch Bowl

Ingredients

½ cup unsweetened coconut milk
1 scoop vanilla whey protein powder
½ cup frozen mixed berries
1–2 tablespoons erythritol
¼ cup granola (for topping)
2 tablespoons shredded coconut (for topping)

Directions

Blend coconut milk, protein powder, berries, and sweetener until creamy.
Pour into a bowl and smooth the top.
Sprinkle granola and shredded coconut over the surface.
Add extra berries for a colorful finish.
Serve immediately for best taste and crunch.

61

Almond Berry Bliss Bowl

Ingredients

½ cup unsweetened almond milk
1 scoop vanilla whey protein powder
½ cup frozen blueberries
½ cup frozen strawberries
1 tablespoon almond butter
1–2 tablespoons monk fruit sweetener

Directions

Blend almond milk, protein powder, blueberries, strawberries, almond butter, and sweetener until thick.
Pour into a serving bowl and level it evenly.
Top with sliced almonds for crunch.
Add a few fresh berries for presentation.
Serve immediately while cold and creamy.

62

Pomegranate Chocolate Bowl

Ingredients

½ cup unsweetened almond milk
1 scoop chocolate whey protein powder
1 tablespoon cocoa powder
1–2 tablespoons monk fruit sweetener
¼ cup pomegranate seeds (plus extra for topping)
2 tablespoons granola (for topping)

Directions

Blend almond milk, protein powder, cocoa powder, sweetener, and half the pomegranate seeds until smooth.
Pour into a bowl and spread evenly.
Sprinkle with granola and remaining pomegranate seeds.
Add a light drizzle of sugar-free chocolate syrup if desired.
Serve immediately for a rich, tangy, and crunchy treat.

Mango Passionfruit Bowl

Ingredients

½ cup unsweetened almond milk
1 scoop vanilla whey protein powder
½ cup frozen mango chunks
¼ cup frozen passionfruit pulp
1–2 tablespoons erythritol
¼ cup coconut flakes (for topping)

Directions

Blend almond milk, protein powder, mango, passionfruit, and sweetener until creamy.
Pour into a serving bowl and smooth the top.
Sprinkle coconut flakes for tropical flair.
Add sliced kiwi for color contrast if desired.
Serve immediately for a refreshing, vitamin-rich treat.

64

Kiwi Banana Bowl

Ingredients

½ cup unsweetened almond milk
1 scoop vanilla whey protein powder
½ frozen banana
½ cup frozen kiwi slices
1–2 tablespoons erythritol
¼ cup granola (for topping)

Directions

Blend almond milk, protein powder, banana, kiwi, and sweetener until thick and creamy.
Scoop into a serving bowl, smoothing the top evenly.
Top with granola for crunch and texture.
Add fresh kiwi slices for presentation.
Serve immediately for a refreshing, tangy-sweet flavor combination.

65

Chia Blueberry Bowl

Ingredients

½ cup unsweetened almond milk
1 scoop vanilla whey protein powder
½ cup frozen blueberries
1 tablespoon chia seeds
1–2 tablespoons monk fruit sweetener
¼ cup shredded coconut (for topping)

Directions

Blend almond milk, protein powder, blueberries, chia seeds, and sweetener until thick.
Transfer to a bowl and level the surface.
Top with shredded coconut for extra flavor.
Add fresh blueberries for garnish if desired.
Serve immediately for a fiber-rich, antioxidant-packed bowl.

66

Raspberry Coconut Bowl

Ingredients

½ cup unsweetened coconut milk
1 scoop vanilla whey protein powder
½ cup frozen raspberries
1–2 tablespoons erythritol
¼ cup granola (for topping)
2 tablespoons shredded coconut (for topping)

Directions

Blend coconut milk, protein powder, raspberries, and sweetener until smooth but thick.
Pour into a bowl, spreading evenly.
Sprinkle with granola and shredded coconut for texture.
Add a few fresh raspberries for color.
Serve immediately for a creamy, tropical berry treat.

67

Peanut Butter Apple Bowl

Ingredients

½ cup unsweetened almond milk
1 scoop vanilla whey protein powder
½ cup frozen apple slices
1 tablespoon peanut butter
1–2 tablespoons monk fruit sweetener
¼ cup granola (for topping)

Directions

Blend almond milk, protein powder, apples, peanut butter, and sweetener until thick and creamy.
Pour into a serving bowl and level it evenly.
Top with granola for crunch.
Garnish with thin apple slices if desired.
Serve immediately for a sweet, nutty apple flavor.

68

Matcha Mango Bowl

Ingredients

½ cup unsweetened almond milk
1 scoop vanilla whey protein powder
1 teaspoon matcha green tea powder
½ cup frozen mango chunks
1–2 tablespoons erythritol
2 tablespoons shredded coconut (for topping)

Directions

Blend almond milk, protein powder, matcha, mango, and sweetener until thick and smooth.
Pour into a serving bowl and smooth the surface.
Top with shredded coconut for texture.
Add mango slices for extra sweetness.
Serve immediately for a tropical matcha delight.

69

Peach Raspberry Bowl

Ingredients

½ cup unsweetened almond milk
1 scoop vanilla whey protein powder
½ cup frozen peaches
½ cup frozen raspberries
1–2 tablespoons monk fruit sweetener
¼ cup granola (for topping)

Directions

Blend almond milk, protein powder, peaches, raspberries, and sweetener until creamy.
Pour into a bowl and level it evenly.
Sprinkle with granola for crunch.
Add fresh peach slices for garnish if desired.
Serve immediately for a fruity, colorful breakfast.

Pineapple Mint Bowl

Ingredients

½ cup unsweetened almond milk
1 scoop vanilla whey protein powder
½ cup frozen pineapple chunks
4–5 fresh mint leaves
1–2 tablespoons erythritol
¼ cup shredded coconut (for topping)

Directions

Blend almond milk, protein powder, pineapple, mint, and sweetener until smooth and aromatic.
Pour into a serving bowl, smoothing the surface.
Top with shredded coconut for a tropical twist.
Add fresh mint sprigs for garnish.
Serve immediately for a cooling, refreshing treat.

70

CHAPTER 6
SORBET RECIPES

71

Lemon Raspberry Sorbet

Ingredients

1 cup water
½ cup frozen raspberries
2 tablespoons lemon juice
1–2 tablespoons erythritol
1 teaspoon lemon zest

Directions

Blend water, raspberries, lemon juice, sweetener, and zest until smooth and vibrant in color.
Pour into the Ninja CREAMi pint, leaving a small gap at the top.
Freeze upright for at least 24 hours until solid.
Process on the "Sorbet" setting until light and airy.
Serve immediately for a tart, refreshing finish, or freeze briefly for a firmer texture.

72

Mango Pineapple Sorbet

Ingredients

1 cup water
½ cup frozen mango chunks
½ cup frozen pineapple chunks
1–2 tablespoons erythritol
1 teaspoon lime juice

Directions

Blend water, mango, pineapple, sweetener, and lime juice until silky smooth.
Transfer mixture into the Ninja CREAMi pint and seal the lid.
Freeze upright for 24 hours before spinning.
Use the "Sorbet" function to process until creamy.
Serve immediately for a tropical treat or chill slightly for firmer scoops.

73

Strawberry Kiwi Sorbet

Ingredients

1 cup water
½ cup frozen strawberries
½ cup frozen kiwi slices
1–2 tablespoons erythritol

Directions

Blend water, strawberries, kiwi, and sweetener until smooth.
Pour into the Ninja CREAMi pint, ensuring it is evenly filled.
Freeze upright for a minimum of 24 hours.
Process on "Sorbet" mode until soft and creamy.
Serve immediately for a tangy-sweet combination that's bright and refreshing.

74

Blood Orange Sorbet

Ingredients

1 cup water
½ cup fresh or frozen blood orange segments
1 teaspoon orange zest
1–2 tablespoons monk fruit sweetener

Directions

Blend water, blood orange, zest, and sweetener until fully combined.
Transfer into Ninja CREAMi pint and secure the lid.
Freeze upright for 24 hours or until solid.
Process on "Sorbet" mode until fluffy and smooth.
Serve immediately for a bold citrus flavor with a hint of sweetness.

Pomegranate Lime Sorbet

Ingredients

1 cup water
½ cup pomegranate seeds
1 tablespoon lime juice
1–2 tablespoons erythritol

Directions

Blend water, pomegranate seeds, lime juice, and sweetener until smooth and vibrant.
Pour mixture into Ninja CREAMi pint and secure lid.
Freeze upright for 24 hours before spinning.
Process on "Sorbet" mode until soft and airy.
Serve immediately for a tangy, antioxidant-rich treat.

76

Blueberry Basil Sorbet

Ingredients

1 cup water
½ cup frozen blueberries
3 fresh basil leaves
1–2 tablespoons erythritol

Directions

Blend water, blueberries, basil, and sweetener until smooth and aromatic.
Pour into Ninja CREAMi pint and close lid tightly.
Freeze upright for 24 hours before spinning.
Process on "Sorbet" mode until light and smooth.
Serve immediately for a unique herbal-fruit pairing.

77

Watermelon Mint Sorbet

Ingredients

1 cup water
1 cup frozen watermelon cubes
4–5 fresh mint leaves
1–2 tablespoons erythritol

Directions

Blend water, watermelon, mint, and sweetener until silky smooth.
Pour into Ninja CREAMi pint, leaving a small gap at the top.
Freeze upright for 24 hours until frozen solid.
Process on "Sorbet" mode until fluffy.
Serve immediately for a cool, summery refreshment.

78

Grapefruit Ginger Sorbet

Ingredients

1 cup water
½ cup grapefruit segments
½ teaspoon grated fresh ginger
1–2 tablespoons monk fruit sweetener

Directions

Blend water, grapefruit, ginger, and sweetener until fully smooth.
Pour mixture into Ninja CREAMi pint and secure lid.
Freeze upright for at least 24 hours.
Process on "Sorbet" mode until creamy.
Serve immediately for a tart, zesty dessert with a hint of spice.

79

Passionfruit Mango Sorbet

Ingredients

1 cup water
½ cup frozen mango chunks
¼ cup passionfruit pulp
1–2 tablespoons erythritol

Directions

Blend water, mango, passionfruit, and sweetener until smooth.
Pour into Ninja CREAMi pint and close lid tightly.
Freeze upright for 24 hours before spinning.
Process on "Sorbet" mode until airy.
Serve immediately for a tropical burst of flavor.

Peach Blackberry Sorbet

Ingredients

1 cup water
½ cup frozen peaches
½ cup frozen blackberries
1–2 tablespoons monk fruit sweetener

Directions

Blend water, peaches, blackberries, and sweetener until smooth.
Transfer mixture to Ninja CREAMi pint and secure lid.
Freeze upright for 24 hours until fully solid.
Process on "Sorbet" setting until creamy.
Serve immediately for a sweet, tangy, and colorful dessert.

81

Cherry Limeade Sorbet

Ingredients

1 cup water
½ cup frozen cherries
1 tablespoon lime juice
1–2 tablespoons monk fruit sweetener

Directions

Blend water, cherries, lime juice, and sweetener until bright and smooth.
Pour into Ninja CREAMi pint and seal with lid.
Freeze upright for 24 hours until fully frozen.
Process on "Sorbet" mode until fluffy.
Serve immediately for a sweet-tart frozen treat.

82

Honeydew Melon Sorbet

Ingredients

1 cup water
1 cup frozen honeydew cubes
1–2 tablespoons erythritol

Directions

Blend water, honeydew, and sweetener until fully smooth and creamy.
Pour into Ninja CREAMi pint and close lid.
Freeze upright for 24 hours before spinning.
Process on "Sorbet" mode until smooth and airy.
Serve immediately for a light, refreshing dessert.

83

Raspberry Lemon Sorbet

Ingredients

1 cup water
½ cup frozen raspberries
2 tablespoons lemon juice
1–2 tablespoons monk fruit sweetener

Directions

Blend water, raspberries, lemon juice, and sweetener until bright and smooth.
Pour into Ninja CREAMi pint and secure lid tightly.
Freeze upright for at least 24 hours.
Process on "Sorbet" mode until fluffy.
Serve immediately for a tangy, vibrant treat.

84

Pineapple Coconut Sorbet

Ingredients

1 cup coconut water
1 cup frozen pineapple chunks
1–2 tablespoons erythritol

Directions

Blend coconut water, pineapple, and sweetener until smooth and tropical.
Pour into Ninja CREAMi pint and secure lid.
Freeze upright for 24 hours before spinning.
Process on "Sorbet" mode until light and fluffy.
Serve immediately for a beach-inspired frozen dessert.

Plum Vanilla Sorbet

Ingredients

1 cup water
½ cup frozen plum slices
½ teaspoon vanilla extract
1–2 tablespoons monk fruit sweetener

Directions

Blend water, plums, vanilla, and sweetener until smooth and fully blended.
Pour into Ninja CREAMi pint and close lid.
Freeze upright for 24 hours until solid.
Process on "Sorbet" mode until creamy.
Serve immediately for a fragrant, slightly tart sorbet.

CHAPTER 7
MIX-IN RECIPES

86

Brownie Bite Protein Ice Cream

Ingredients

1 cup unsweetened almond milk
1 scoop chocolate whey protein powder
1 tablespoon cocoa powder
1–2 tablespoons monk fruit sweetener
3 tablespoons sugar-free brownie chunks

Directions

Blend almond milk, protein powder, cocoa powder, and sweetener until smooth.
Pour into Ninja CREAMi pint and secure lid.
Freeze upright for 24 hours until solid.
Process on "Ice Cream" mode until creamy.
Fold in brownie chunks using Mix-In, then serve immediately for a rich chocolate indulgence.

87

Cookie Dough Power Pint

Ingredients

1 cup unsweetened almond milk
1 scoop vanilla whey protein powder
1 teaspoon vanilla extract
1–2 tablespoons erythritol
3 tablespoons sugar-free cookie dough pieces

Directions

Blend almond milk, protein powder, vanilla extract, and sweetener until fully smooth.
Transfer to Ninja CREAMi pint and secure lid tightly.
Freeze upright for at least 24 hours before processing.
Use "Ice Cream" mode to process until creamy.
Add cookie dough using Mix-In and serve immediately for the best texture.

Peanut Butter Cup Swirl

Ingredients

1 cup unsweetened almond milk
1 scoop chocolate whey protein powder
1 tablespoon cocoa powder
1–2 tablespoons monk fruit sweetener
3 tablespoons chopped sugar-free peanut butter cups

Directions

Blend almond milk, protein powder, cocoa, and sweetener until smooth.
Pour into Ninja CREAMi pint and secure lid.
Freeze upright for 24 hours before spinning.
Process on "Ice Cream" mode until creamy.
Mix in peanut butter cup pieces, then serve soft or after a brief freezer chill.

88

89

S'mores Protein Cream

Ingredients

1 cup unsweetened almond milk
1 scoop chocolate whey protein powder
1 tablespoon cocoa powder
1–2 tablespoons monk fruit sweetener
2 tablespoons crushed sugar-free graham crackers
2 tablespoons sugar-free mini marshmallows

Directions

Blend almond milk, protein powder, cocoa, and sweetener until fully combined.
Pour into Ninja CREAMi pint and secure lid.
Freeze upright for 24 hours before processing.
Process on "Ice Cream" mode until creamy.
Fold in graham crackers and marshmallows using Mix-In, then serve immediately.

90

Caramel Pretzel Delight

Ingredients

1 cup unsweetened almond milk
1 scoop caramel-flavored whey protein powder
1–2 tablespoons monk fruit sweetener
3 tablespoons crushed pretzels

Directions

Blend almond milk, protein powder, and sweetener until smooth.
Transfer to Ninja CREAMi pint and secure lid.
Freeze upright for at least 24 hours.
Process on "Ice Cream" mode until creamy.
Add pretzel pieces with Mix-In for a sweet-salty crunch and serve.

Berry Crunch Yogurt Mix-In

Ingredients

1 cup plain unsweetened Greek yogurt
1 scoop vanilla whey protein powder
1–2 tablespoons erythritol
3 tablespoons mixed berry granola

Directions

Blend yogurt, protein powder, and sweetener until smooth and creamy.
Transfer to Ninja CREAMi pint and seal lid.
Freeze upright for 24 hours before processing.
Use "Lite Ice Cream" mode for a yogurt-like texture.
Fold in granola for a crunchy finish and serve immediately.

91

92

Almond Biscotti Crunch

Ingredients

1 cup unsweetened almond milk
1 scoop vanilla whey protein powder
1 teaspoon almond extract
1–2 tablespoons erythritol
3 tablespoons chopped sugar-free almond biscotti

Directions

Blend almond milk, protein powder, almond extract, and sweetener until smooth.
Pour into Ninja CREAMi pint and close lid tightly.
Freeze upright for 24 hours before processing.
Process on "Ice Cream" mode until creamy.
Fold in biscotti pieces using Mix-In, then serve immediately.

93

Apple Crumble Swirl

Ingredients

1 cup unsweetened almond milk
1 scoop vanilla whey protein powder
1 teaspoon cinnamon
1–2 tablespoons monk fruit sweetener
3 tablespoons sugar-free crumble topping

Directions

Blend almond milk, protein powder, cinnamon, and sweetener until fully smooth.
Pour into Ninja CREAMi pint and seal lid.
Freeze upright for 24 hours before spinning.
Process on "Lite Ice Cream" mode until creamy.
Fold in crumble topping using Mix-In for a dessert-like finish.

Mocha Espresso Chip

Ingredients

1 cup unsweetened almond milk
1 scoop chocolate whey protein powder
1 teaspoon instant espresso powder
1–2 tablespoons monk fruit sweetener
3 tablespoons sugar-free chocolate chips

Directions

Blend almond milk, protein powder, espresso powder, and sweetener until smooth.
Transfer to Ninja CREAMi pint and secure lid.
Freeze upright for 24 hours before spinning.
Process on "Ice Cream" mode until creamy.
Add chocolate chips with Mix-In, then serve immediately.

95

Banana Nut Brownie Swirl

Ingredients

1 cup unsweetened almond milk
1 scoop chocolate whey protein powder
½ ripe banana
1–2 tablespoons monk fruit sweetener
3 tablespoons sugar-free brownie chunks

Directions

Blend almond milk, protein powder, banana, and sweetener until smooth.
Transfer to Ninja CREAMi pint and secure lid.
Freeze upright for at least 24 hours.
Process on "Ice Cream" mode until creamy.
Add brownie chunks with Mix-In, then serve for a decadent finish.

96

Hazelnut Chocolate Ripple

Ingredients

1 cup unsweetened almond milk
1 scoop chocolate whey protein powder
1 tablespoon cocoa powder
1–2 tablespoons monk fruit sweetener
3 tablespoons sugar-free hazelnut spread

Directions

Blend almond milk, protein powder, cocoa, and sweetener until smooth.
Pour into Ninja CREAMi pint and secure lid.
Freeze upright for at least 24 hours.
Process on "Ice Cream" mode until creamy.
Swirl in hazelnut spread after spinning, then serve immediately.

95

Cinnamon Roll Cookie Crunch

Ingredients

1 cup unsweetened oat milk
1 scoop vanilla whey protein powder
1 teaspoon cinnamon
1–2 tablespoons erythritol
3 tablespoons chopped sugar-free cookies

Directions

Blend oat milk, protein powder, cinnamon, and sweetener until fully smooth.
Pour into Ninja CREAMi pint and close lid securely.
Freeze upright for 24 hours before processing.
Use "Lite Ice Cream" mode for a lighter texture.
Fold in cookie pieces using Mix-In, then serve.

98

Strawberry Shortcake Bits

Ingredients

1 cup unsweetened almond milk
1 scoop vanilla whey protein powder
1–2 tablespoons erythritol
3 tablespoons chopped sugar-free shortcake pieces
¼ cup diced strawberries

Directions

Blend almond milk, protein powder, and sweetener until fully smooth.
Pour into Ninja CREAMi pint and secure lid tightly.
Freeze upright for 24 hours before processing.
Use "Lite Ice Cream" mode for a lighter texture.
Mix in shortcake pieces and strawberries using Mix-In, then serve.

99

Pistachio Cranberry Clusters

Ingredients

1 cup unsweetened almond milk
1 scoop vanilla whey protein powder
1 teaspoon pistachio extract
1–2 tablespoons erythritol
3 tablespoons pistachio-cranberry mix

Directions

Blend almond milk, protein powder, pistachio extract, and sweetener until smooth.
Pour into Ninja CREAMi pint and seal lid securely.
Freeze upright for 24 hours before spinning.
Process on "Ice Cream" mode until creamy.
Fold in pistachio-cranberry mix using Mix-In, then serve.

Tropical Granola Crunch

Ingredients

1 cup unsweetened coconut milk
1 scoop vanilla whey protein powder
1–2 tablespoons monk fruit sweetener
3 tablespoons tropical granola mix

Directions

Blend coconut milk, protein powder, and sweetener until fully combined.
Pour into Ninja CREAMi pint and close lid tightly.
Freeze upright for 24 hours before processing.
Use "Lite Ice Cream" mode for a lighter texture.
Mix in granola with Mix-In, then serve for a tropical crunch.